FOR SHERWOOD AND STRASBURGER

Acknowledgments

I would like to thank educators Candise Stiewing and Maggie Siena for their insight and advice. I thank David, Aidan, and Olive for their constant support and encouragement. And I am deeply grateful to Lee Wade and Anne Schwartz, with whom it is always a perfect pleasure to collaborate.

Visit us on the Web! www.randomhouse.com/kids
Educators and librarians, for a variety of teaching tools,
visit us at www.randomhouse.com/teachers

Library of Congress Cataloging-in-Publication Data
Fisher, Valorie.
Everything I need to know before I'm five / Valorie Fisher. — 1st ed.
    p. cm.
ISBN 978-0-375-86865-8 (hc) — ISBN 978-0-375-96865-5 (glb)
1. Number concept—Juvenile literature. 2. Polarity—Juvenile literature. 3. Geometry—Juvenile literature. 4. Colors—Juvenile literature. 5. Seasons—Juvenile literature.
6. Alphabets—Juvenile literature. I. Title.
QA40.5.F57 2011
[E]—dc22
2010031265

The text of this book is set in Monod Brun.
The illustrations are assemblages of toys, paper and wood cutouts, and other found treasures photographed with a digital camera.

MANUFACTURED IN CHINA
10 9 8 7 6 5 4 3 2
First Edition

EVERYTHING
I NEED TO KNOW BEFORE I'M FIVE

valorie fisher

schwartz & wade books • new york

NUMBERS

one **1**

two **2**

three **3**

4 four

five 5

6
six

7 seven

eight

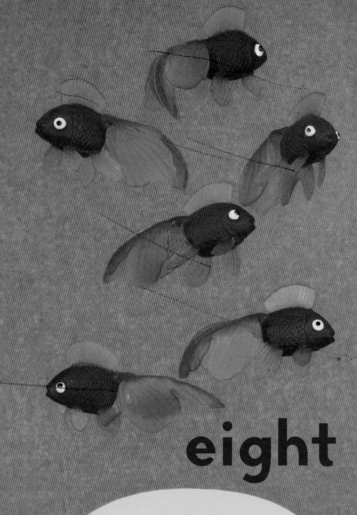

nine

10 ten

NUMBERS

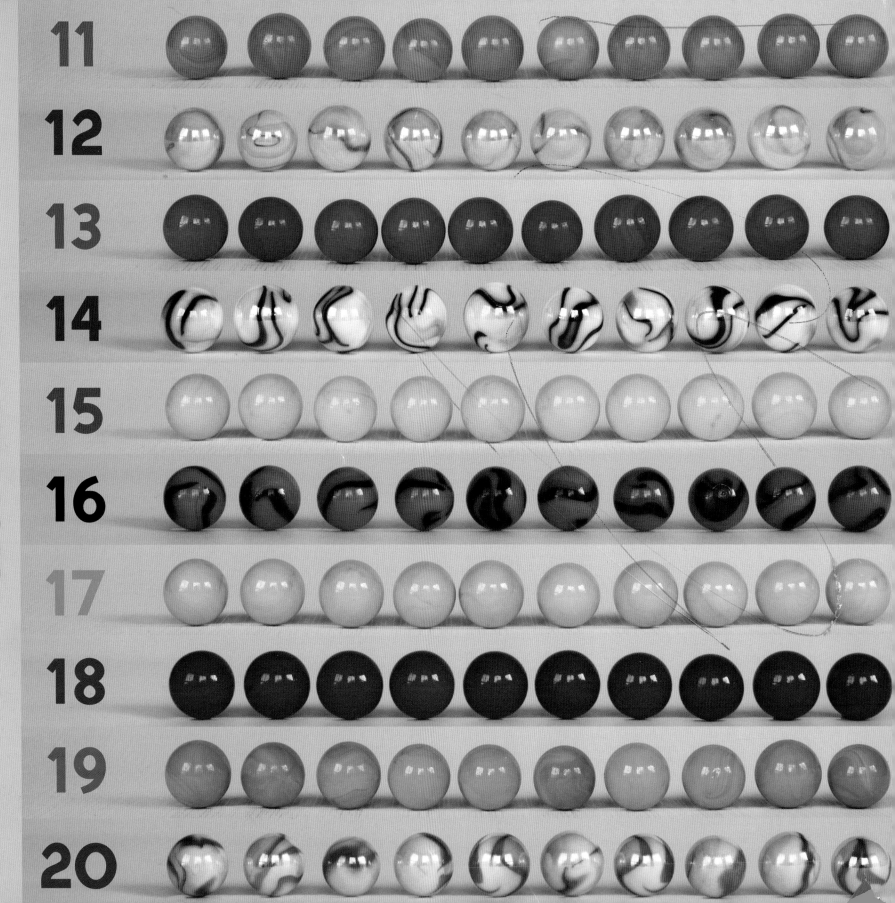

NUMBERS

11
12
13
14
15
16
17
18
19
20

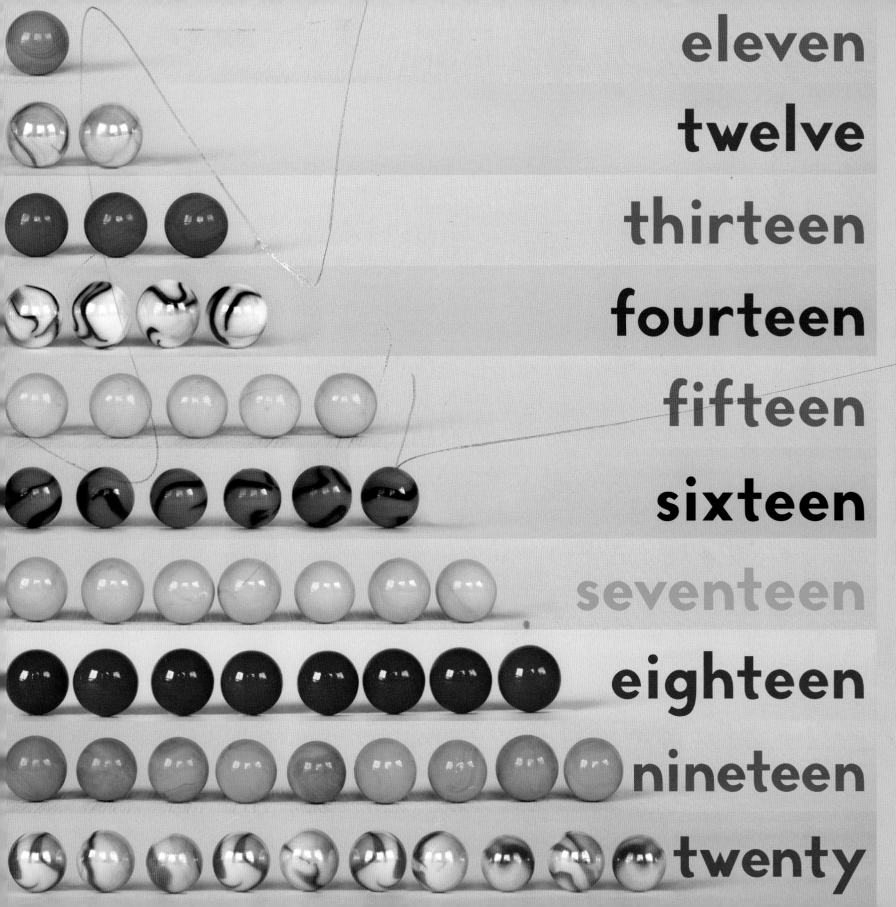

eleven

twelve

thirteen

fourteen

fifteen

sixteen

seventeen

eighteen

nineteen

twenty

NUMBERS

OPPOSITES

little

big

easy

hard

OPPOSITES

full

empty

in

out

OPPOSITES

push pull

open

shut

up   down   happy   sad

long   short   off   on

OPPOSITES

SHAPES

square

triangle

circle

heart

star

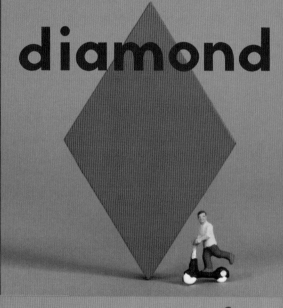
diamond

hexagon

oval

rectangle

cylinder

cone

sphere

cube

SHAPES

RED

YELLOW

BLUE

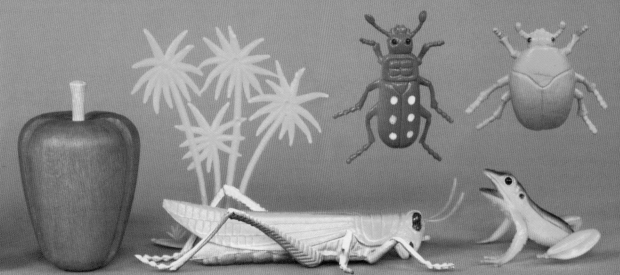

GREEN

PURPLE

ORANGE

BLACK WHITE

COLORS

 +  =

 +  =

 +  =

 +  =

 +  =

SEASONS

spring

summer

fall

winter

sunny

windy

cloudy

rainy

stormy

snowy

WEATHER

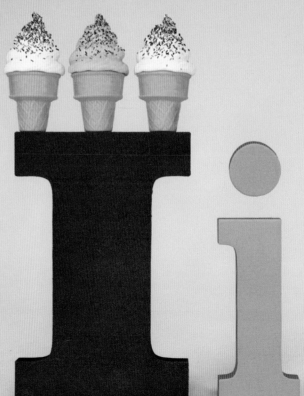

ALPHABET